TREATS

just great recipes

GENERAL INFORMATION

The level of difficulty of the recipes in this book
is expressed as a number from 1 (simple) to 3 (difficult).

TREATS
just great recipes

pasta
sauces

M<small>c</small>RAE BOOKS

SERVES 4–6

PREPARATION 10 min

COOKING 45 min

DIFFICULTY level 1

Tomato Sauce
with sausage and pecorino

Heat the oil in a large frying pan over medium heat. Add the sausages, onion, garlic, and torn basil and sauté until the onion turns pale gold, about 5 minutes. • Add the tomatoes and season with salt and pepper. Simmer for 15–20 minutes, or until the sauce thickens and reduces. • Cook the pasta in a large pan of salted boiling water until al dente. • Drain well and add to the pan with the sauce. Sprinkle with the pecorino and toss gently. • Garnish with the extra basil and serve hot.

¼ cup (60 ml) extra-virgin olive oil

14 oz (400 g) Italian pork sausages, skinned and crumbled

1 large onion, finely chopped

3 cloves garlic, finely chopped

8 basil leaves, torn + extra to garnish

1½ lb (750 g) tomatoes, peeled and chopped

Salt and freshly ground black pepper

⅓ cup (45 g) freshly grated pecorino cheese

1 lb (500 g) malloreddus, penne or other short pasta shape

Gorgonzola Sauce

Cook the pasta in a large pan of salted boiling water until al dente. • While the pasta is cooking, stir the butter, gorgonzola, and cream in a double boiler over barely simmering water until the cheese has melted. Season with salt. • Drain the pasta and transfer to a heated serving dish. • Pour the gorgonzola sauce over the top, sprinkle with the Parmesan, and toss gently. • Serve hot.

2 tablespoons butter

14 oz (400 g) creamy gorgonzola cheese, crumbled

¾ cup (180 ml) heavy (double) cream

Salt

1 lb (500 g) penne or other short pasta shape

½ cup (60 g) freshly grated Parmesan cheese

Bell Pepper Sauce

Cut the bell peppers in half, remove the stalks and seeds, and cut into thin strips. • Heat the oil in a large frying pan over medium heat. Sauté the bell peppers, pancetta, onion, and garlic for 8–10 minutes. • Add the boiling water and season with salt and pepper. Simmer for about 20 minutes, or until the bell peppers are tender. • Stir in the vinegar and cook over high heat for 2–3 minutes until the vinegar evaporates. Remove from the heat. • Meanwhile, cook the pasta in a large pan of salted, boiling water until al dente. Drain well and place in a heated serving dish. • Pour the sauce over the top, sprinkle with the cheese, and toss well. • Serve hot.

3 large yellow bell peppers (capsicums)
⅓ cup (90 ml) extra-virgin olive oil
⅔ cup (150 g) pancetta, diced
1 large onion, finely chopped
2 cloves garlic, finely chopped
3 tablespoons boiling water
Salt and freshly ground black pepper
2 tablespoons white wine vinegar
1 lb (500 g) penne penne or other
     short pasta shape
½ cup (60 g) freshly grated Parmesan
     cheese

SERVES 4

PREPARATION 15 min

COOKING 1 h 15 min

DIFFICULTY level 2

Lamb Sauce
with pecorino

Sauté the garlic in the oil in a large saucepan over medium heat until the garlic turns pale gold. • Add the lamb, pork, and bay leaves and sauté until the meat is browned all over. • Stir in the tomatoes, basil, and marjoram. Season with salt and pepper. Simmer over low heat for 1 hour. • Cook the pasta in a large pot of salted boiling water until al dente. • Drain the pasta and transfer to a heated serving dish. Toss carefully with the sauce. If preferred, discard the bay leaves before serving. • Sprinkle with the pecorino and serve hot.

4 cloves garlic, finely chopped

$1/3$ cup (90 ml) extra-virgin olive oil

1 lb (500 g) ground (minced) lamb

5 oz (150 g) ground (minced) lean pork

2 bay leaves

$1^1/2$ lb (750 g) tomatoes, peeled, and chopped

8 leaves fresh basil

1 tablespoon finely chopped fresh marjoram

Salt and freshly ground black pepper

14 oz (400 g) maltagliati, tagliatelle, or other fresh pasta

$1/2$ cup (60 g) freshly grated pecorino cheese

SERVES 6

PREPARATION 20 min + 1 h to drain

COOKING 50 min

DIFFICULTY level 1

Tomato Sauce
Naples-style

Cook the tomatoes with ½ teaspoon salt in a covered saucepan over medium heat for 5 minutes. • Transfer to a colander with large holes and let drain for 1 hour. • Return to the saucepan and add the onion, garlic, basil, oil, sugar, and salt. Cover and bring to a boil over medium heat. Simmer for about 40 minutes, or until the sauce has thickened. • Remove from the heat and run through a food mill or process in a food processor or blender until smooth. • Cook the pasta in a large pan of salted boiling water until al dente. Drain well and transfer to a heated serving dish. • Pour the sauce over the top. Toss well and serve hot.

3 lb (1.5 kg) firm-ripe plum tomatoes, coarsely chopped
Salt
1 red onion, thinly sliced
2 cloves garlic, finely chopped
Leaves from 1 small bunch fresh basil, torn
2 tablespoons extra-virgin olive oil
½ teaspoon sugar
1 lb (500 g) short or long dried pasta

Tomato Sauce
with onion and pancetta

Heat the oil in a large frying pan over medium heat. Sauté the onions for 5 minutes. Add the pancetta and sauté for 5 more minutes. • Add the tomatoes and simmer for 10 minutes. • Pour in the wine, season with salt and pepper, and simmer for 10 more minutes. • Cover and simmer over low heat for about 1 hour, stirring frequently. • Cook the pasta in a large pan of salted boiling water until al dente. Drain well and transfer to a heated serving dish. • Pour the sauce over the top. Toss well and serve hot.

$\frac{1}{4}$ cup (60 ml) extra-virgin olive oil
$1\frac{1}{4}$ lb (600 g) onions, thinly sliced
5 oz (150 g) pancetta, diced
1 lb (500 g) ripe tomatoes, peeled and chopped
$\frac{1}{2}$ cup (125 ml) dry red wine
Salt and freshly ground black pepper
1 lb (500 g) bucatini or spaghetti

SERVES 4–6

PREPARATION 15 min + 15 min to soak

COOKING 30 min

DIFFICULTY level 1

Spicy Tuna Sauce
with mushrooms and pancetta

Soak the mushrooms in ½ cup (125 ml) of warm water for 15 minutes. Drain well, reserving the liquid. Chop the drained mushrooms finely. • Heat the oil in a large frying pan over medium heat. Add the pancetta, garlic, and chile peppers. Sauté until the garlic is pale golden brown, 2–3 minutes. • Add the mushrooms and tomatoes and sauté until reduced, about 10 minutes. Add a little of the reserved soaking liquid and let it evaporate. • Stir in the tuna. Mix well and season with salt. Lower the heat and simmer for 5 minutes. • Meanwhile, cook the pasta in a large pot of salted boiling water until al dente. Drain well and transfer to the frying pan with the sauce. Add a little more of the mushroom liquid if the sauce is too thick. • Toss over high heat for 1 minute and season with pepper. • Garnish with the parsley and serve hot.

1 oz (30 g) dried mushrooms

⅓ cup (90 ml) extra-virgin olive oil

⅔ cup (75 g) chopped pancetta

2 cloves garlic, finely chopped

2 dried chilies, crumbled

4 large tomatoes, peeled and chopped

4 oz (125 g) canned tuna, drained and crumbled

Salt and freshly ground black pepper

1 lb (500 g) spaghetti or other long dried pasta shape

2 tablespoons finely chopped fresh parsley

SERVES 4–6

PREPARATION 20 min + 1 h to soak

COOKING 30 min

DIFFICULTY level 1

Spicy Clam Sauce

Soak the clams in cold water for 1 hour. • Place the clams in a large pan over medium heat with a little water. Cook until they open, 5–10 minutes. Discard any clams that do not open. Remove from the heat and discard most of the clam shells. Leave a few mollusks in their shells to garnish. • Heat the oil in a large frying pan over medium heat. Add the garlic and chile and sauté until lightly browned, about 3 minutes. • Add the tomatoes and wine, season with salt, and simmer until the tomatoes begin to break down, about 15 minutes. Add the clams and stir well. • Meanwhile, cook the pasta in a large pot of salted boiling water until al dente. Drain and add to the pan with the clams. Toss over high heat for 2 minutes. • Sprinkle with the parsley and serve hot.

2 lb (1 kg) clams, in shell
1/3 cup (90 ml) extra-virgin olive oil
4 cloves garlic, finely chopped
1 fresh red chile, seeded and chopped
6 large tomatoes, sliced
1/3 cup (90 ml) dry white wine
Salt
1 lb (500 g) spaghetti or other dried long pasta shape
3 tablespoons finely chopped fresh parsley

Garlic Sauce

Sauté the garlic in the oil in a small saucepan over low heat until it turns pale gold. • Stir in the tomatoes, chile, and salt. Simmer over low heat for 40 minutes. Season with salt. • Meanwhile, cook the pasta in a large pot of salted boiling water until al dente. Drain and add to the pan with the sauce. Toss over high heat for 2 minutes. • Serve hot.

10 cloves garlic, lightly crushed but whole

5 tablespoons extra-virgin olive oil

2 lb (1 kg) tomatoes, peeled, seeded, and finely chopped

1 dried red chile, crumbled

Salt

1 lb (500 g) spaghetti or other dried long pasta shape

Pesto Sauce
with potatoes and green beans

Cook the green beans in a large pot of salted boiling water until almost tender, 4–5 minutes. Drain and set aside. • Pesto: Chop the basil, garlic, and pine nuts in a food processor. Gradually add the oil as you chop. • Transfer to a small bowl. Stir in the cheese and season with salt and pepper. • Cook the pasta in a large pot of salted boiling water for 5 minutes. Add the potatoes and cook until the pasta is al dente and the potatoes are tender, about 7–8 minutes more. • Drain well, reserving 2 tablespoons of the cooking liquid. Place the pasta and potatoes in a heated serving bowl. • Add the reserved cooking liquid to the pesto. Pour the pesto into the pasta and potatoes, add the green beans, and toss well. • Season with pepper. Serve hot.

14 oz (400 g) green beans, cut in short lengths

Pesto
1 large bunch fresh basil leaves
2 cloves garlic
3 tablespoons pine nuts
1/2 cup (125 ml) extra-virgin olive oil
Salt and freshly ground black pepper
6 tablespoons freshly grated pecorino cheese

1 lb (500 g) linguine or other dried long pasta shape
8 new potatoes, cut into small cubes

SERVES 4–6

PREPARATION 10 min

COOKING 15 min

DIFFICULTY level 1

Tomato Sauce
with fresh lemon

Blanch the tomatoes in boiling water for 2 minutes. Drain and peel them. Chop coarsely. • Cook the pasta in a large pot of salted boiling water until al dente. • Drain well and transfer to a large serving dish. • Add the tomatoes, basil, oil, lemon juice, and garlic. Season with salt and pepper. Toss well. • Garnish with basil and serve hot.

2 lb (1 kg) ripe tomatoes

1 lb (500 g) spaghetti or other dried long pasta shape

4 tablespoons finely chopped fresh basil + extra leaves, to garnish

$1/3$ cup (90 ml) extra-virgin olive oil

Freshly squeezed juice of 1 lemon

2 cloves garlic, finely chopped

Salt and freshly ground black pepper

Artichoke Sauce

Remove the tough outer leaves from the artichokes by snapping them off at the base. Cut off the top third of the remaining leaves. Cut the artichokes in half, removing any fuzzy choke with a sharp knife. Rub with the lemon. • Thinly slice the artichokes vertically and put them in a large saucepan with the oil and onion. Cover and simmer over medium heat for 10 minutes. • Add the mushrooms, garlic, and parsley and sauté for 3 minutes. • Increase the heat and pour in the wine and tomato. Bring to a boil and simmer for 10 minutes. • Stir in the butter and season with salt and pepper. • Cook the pasta in a large pot of salted boiling water until al dente. • Drain well and transfer to the pan with the sauce. Toss well and serve hot.

3 medium artichokes

1 lemon

$1/4$ cup (60 ml) extra-virgin olive oil

1 onion, finely chopped

$1/2$ oz (15 g) dried mushrooms, soaked in warm water for 15 minutes, drained, and coarsely chopped

2 cloves garlic, finely chopped

1 tablespoon finely chopped fresh parsley

$1/4$ cup (60 ml) dry white wine

1 large tomato, peeled and chopped

1 tablespoon butter

Salt and freshly ground black pepper

1 lb (500 g) fusilli or other dried short pasta shape

Walnut Sauce

Melt the butter with the garlic in a frying pan over medium heat. Sauté for 1 minute, then add the walnuts. • Continue cooking for 2 minutes and mix in the cream. • Cook over low heat until the sauce thickens, about 12 minutes. Season with salt and pepper. • Cook the pasta in a large pot of salted boiling water until al dente. • Drain well and transfer heated serving bowl. Add the sauce. Toss carefully and serve hot.

3 tablespoons butter
3 cloves garlic, finely chopped
50 walnuts, coarsely crushed
1 cup (250 ml) heavy (double) cream
Salt and freshly ground white pepper
1 lb (500 g) farfalle or other dried
   short pasta shape

SERVES 4–6

PREPARATION 15 min

COOKING 15 min

DIFFICULTY level 1

Basil-Walnut Sauce

Crush the basil with the walnuts in a pestle and mortar or chop them finely in a food processor. • Transfer to a serving bowl and add 3 tablespoons of pecorino. Season with salt and pepper. • Pour in the oil and mix until creamy. • Cook the pasta in a large pot of salted boiling water until al dente. Drain and transfer to the serving bowl. • Sprinkle with the remaining pecorino and serve hot.

1 large bunch fresh basil
1 cup (150 g) walnuts
1 cup (125 g) freshly grated pecorino cheese
Salt and freshly ground black pepper
$1/3$ cup (90 ml) extra-virgin olive oil
1 lb (500 g) dried bavette, linguine, or spaghetti

Chicken
liver sauce

Soak the chicken livers in the water and vinegar for 15 minutes. Drain. • Heat the butter and oil with the sage in a medium saucepan over low heat. • Add the chicken livers and sauté over high heat for 2–3 minutes, until browned all over. Season with salt and pepper. • Remove the chicken livers and coarsely chop. Return the chicken livers to the saucepan and pour in the stock. Simmer over high heat for 5 minutes, or until the sauce has reduced by half. • Cook the pasta in a large pot of salted boiling water until al dente. • Drain and add to the sauce. Sprinkle with the Parmesan and serve hot.

1 lb (500 g) chicken livers, trimmed
$\frac{1}{2}$ cup (125 ml) water
$\frac{1}{2}$ cup (125 ml) white wine vinegar
$\frac{1}{4}$ cup (60 g) butter
3 tablespoons extra-virgin olive oil
3 leaves fresh sage, finely chopped
Salt and freshly ground white pepper
$\frac{3}{4}$ cup (180 ml) chicken stock
(homemade or bouillon cube)
1 lb (500 g) spaghetti or tagliatelle
$\frac{3}{4}$ cup (90 g) freshly grated Parmesan cheese

Radicchio Sauce
with sausage

Sauté the garlic in the oil in a large frying pan over medium heat for 3 minutes, until pale gold. • Discard the garlic. Add the sausages and sauté for 3 minutes, until browned all over. • Add the onion and cook for 10 minutes, until soft and golden. • Add the radicchio and cook for 3 minutes. • Meanwhile, cook the pasta in a large pot of salted boiling water for 2–3 minutes, until al dente. • Drain and add to the sauce. Toss well and serve hot.

1 clove garlic, lightly crushed but whole
1/4 cup (60 ml) extra-virgin olive oil
2 Italian sausages, peeled and crumbled
1/2 onion, finely chopped
1 lb (500 g) Treviso radicchio or red chicory, shredded
1 lb (500 g) fresh lasagne sheets or tagliatelle

SERVES 6–8

PREPARATION 30 min

COOKING 3 h 30 min

DIFFICULTY level 1

Tuscan Meat Ragù

Finely chop the carrots, celery, and onions together. • Heat the oil in a medium saucepan and add the vegetables. Sauté over medium-low heat for 10 minutes. • Add the garlic and parsley and cook for 10 minutes more. • Increase the heat to medium-high, add the beef, and sauté until brown all over, 2–3 minutes. • Pour in the wine and add the tomatoes, bay leaf, rosemary, and lemon. Season with salt and pepper. • Cover and simmer over very low heat for about 3 hours, adding water if the mixture starts to dry. Remove the bay leaf and lemon zest before serving. • Cook the pasta in a large pot of salted boiling water until al dente. • Drain and add to the sauce. Toss gently and serve hot.

2 carrots, chopped
2 stalks celery, chopped
2 red onions, chopped
²⁄₃ cup (150 ml) extra-virgin olive oil
2 cloves garlic, chopped
2 tablespoons finely chopped fresh parsley
12 oz (300 g) lean ground (minced) beef
¾ cup (200 ml) dry red wine
2 lb (1 kg) peeled plum tomatoes, pressed through a fine mesh strainer (passata)
1 bay leaf
1 sprig fresh rosemary, finely chopped
Small piece lemon zest
Salt and freshly ground black pepper
Water (optional)
1 lb (500 g) short or long pasta

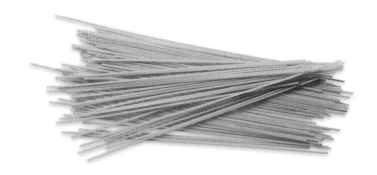

SERVES 4

PREPARATION 20 min

COOKING 20 min

DIFFICULTY level I

Pancetta Sauce
with onion, tomato, and cheese

Sauté the pancetta in the oil in a saucepan over medium heat until lightly browned, about 5 minutes. Remove the pancetta and set aside. • Sauté the onion in the same saucepan for 3 minutes, until softened. • Add the tomatoes and cook over high heat for about 5 minutes, until they soften and begin to thicken. Add the pancetta. • Cook for 5 minutes, add the marjoram, and remove from the heat. Season with salt and pepper. • Meanwhile, cook the pasta in a large pot of salted boiling water until al dente. • Drain well. Serve with the sauce and sprinkle with pecorino.

- 1¾ cups (200 g) pancetta, cut into small cubes
- 2 tablespoons extra-virgin olive oil
- 1 red onion, finely chopped
- 14 oz (400 g) tomatoes, peeled, seeded, and coarsely chopped
- Leaves from 1 small bunch fresh marjoram, finely chopped
- Salt and freshly ground black pepper
- 1 lb (500 g) spaghetti or other dried long pasta shape
- ½ cup (60 g) freshly grated pecorino cheese

Spicy Sauce
with tomato and chile

Sauté the garlic, parsley, and chile in the oil in a large frying pan over medium heat for 2 minutes, until the garlic is pale gold. • Stir in the tomatoes and cook over high heat until the tomatoes have broken down, about 10 minutes. • Season with salt and remove from the heat. • Meanwhile, cook the pasta in a large pot of salted boiling water until al dente. • Drain and add to the sauce. Cook over high heat, stirring until the sauce sticks to the pasta. Serve hot.

2 cloves garlic, finely chopped,
1 tablespoon finely chopped fresh parsley
1 fresh red chile, finely chopped
1/3 cup (90 ml) extra-virgin olive oil
1 lb (500 g) firm-ripe tomatoes, peeled and coarsely chopped
Salt
1 lb (500 g) whole-wheat (wholemeal) spaghetti or other dried long pasta shape

Spicy Sauce
with garlic, oil, and chile

Cook the pasta in a large pot of salted boiling water until al dente. • Drain and transfer to a large heated serving bowl. • Heat the oil with the garlic and chilies in a small saucepan over low heat for 3 minutes, until the garlic is just beginning to turn pale gold. • Drizzle the spicy oil over the pasta and sprinkle with parsley. Toss gently and serve hot.

1 tablespoon finely chopped fresh parsley

1/2 cup (125 ml) extra-virgin olive oil

6 cloves garlic, finely chopped

2 fresh red chilies, finely chopped

3 tablespoons finely chopped fresh parsley

1 lb (500 g) spaghetti or other dried long pasta shape

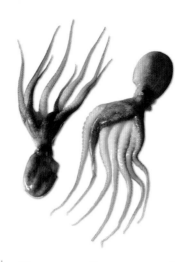

SERVES 4–6

PREPARATION 20 min

COOKING 20 min

DIFFICULTY level 2

Seafood Sauce

Sauté the garlic in the oil in a large frying pan over medium heat until pale gold, about 3 minutes. • Add the squid and half the scampi and sauté over high heat for 5 minutes. • Pour in the wine and simmer until evaporated, for 2–3 minutes. • Season with salt and remove from the heat. • Cook the pasta in a large pot of salted boiling water until not quite al dente. • Blanch the remaining scampi in the pot with the pasta water until cooked, for 3–4 minutes. • Remove the scampi with a slotted spoon and set aside. Drain the pasta and add to the frying pan with the sauce. • Transfer to a serving plate, garnish with the blanched scampi, and sprinkle with parsley. Serve hot.

2 cloves garlic, finely chopped

5 tablespoons extra-virgin olive oil

8 oz (250 g) small squid cut into thin rings and with tentacles split in half

6 large Dublin Bay prawns or jumbo shrimp (about 8 oz/250 g) in total), cut in half lengthwise with kitchen shears

1/4 cup (60 ml) dry white wine

Salt

1 lb (500 g) dried capellini, spaghettini, or angel hair pasta

2 tablespoons finely chopped fresh parsley

SERVES 4

PREPARATION 40 min +12 h to dry pasta

COOKING 55 min

DIFFICULTY level 3

Vegetable Sauce
with homemade spaghetti

Pasta Dough: Sift the flour and salt into a mound on a clean work surface and make a well in the center. Mix in enough water to make a smooth dough. Knead for 15–20 minutes, until smooth and elastic. Shape the dough into a ball, wrap in plastic wrap (cling film), and let rest for 30 minutes. • Break off pieces of dough and roll into 6 x $\frac{1}{8}$-inch (15-cm x 3-mm) lengths. Let dry on a flour-dusted cloth overnight to prevent them from sticking together. • Sauce: Put the onion, carrot, and celery in the oil in a large frying pan over medium heat. Season with salt. Cover and simmer over low heat until the vegetables are very soft, about 15 minutes. • Add the garlic, parsley, and chile and sauté over high heat for 1 minute. • Stir in the tomatoes and simmer over low heat for 30 minutes. Season with salt. • Cook the pasta in a large pot of salted boiling water until al dente, 3–4 minutes. • Drain and add to the sauce. Sprinkle with the pecorino and serve.

Pasta Dough
$2\frac{1}{3}$ cups (350 g) all-purpose (plain) flour
$\frac{1}{4}$ teaspoon salt
Lukewarm water

Sauce
1 large red onion, finely chopped
1 carrot, finely chopped
1 stalk celery, finely chopped
$\frac{1}{3}$ cup (90 ml) extra-virgin oil
Salt
2 cloves garlic, finely chopped
1 tablespoon finely chopped fresh parsley
1 fresh red chile pepper, finely chopped
2 (14-oz/400-g) cans tomatoes, with juice
6 tablespoons freshly grated pecorino romano cheese

Fettuccine Sauce

Sauté the onion, carrot, and celery in the oil in a large saucepan over medium heat until the onion is lightly browned, about 5 minutes. • Add the beef and sauté until browned all over. • Increase the heat and pour in the wine. • Add the chicken livers and simmer over low heat for 15 minutes. • Add the tomatoes, mushrooms, and bay leaf and season with salt and pepper. Simmer over low heat for about 1 hour. • Cook the pasta in a large pot of salted boiling water until al dente. • Drain and add to the sauce. Sprinkle with the Parmesan, dot with the butter, and serve hot.

1 red onion, finely chopped

1 small carrot, finely chopped

1 small stalk celery, finely chopped

1/4 cup (60 ml) extra-virgin olive oil

8 oz (250 g) lean ground (minced) beef

1/3 cup (90 ml) dry red wine

4 oz (100 g) chicken livers, trimmed and diced

1 (14-oz/400-g) can tomatoes, with juice

1/2 oz (15 g) dried porcini mushrooms, soaked in warm water for 15 minutes and finely chopped

1 bay leaf

Salt and freshly ground black pepper

14 oz (400 g) fettuccine o tagliatelle

1 cup (125 g) freshly grated Parmesan cheese

1/4 cup (60 g) butter, cut up

SERVES 4–6

PREPARATION 10 min

COOKING 25 min

DIFFICULTY level 1

Pancetta Sauce
with onion and pecorino

Sauté the pancetta in the oil in a small frying pan over low heat for 5 minutes. • Remove from the pan and set aside. • Add the onion to the same oil and sauté for 10–15 minutes, or until soft. Return the pancetta to the pan, increase the heat, and pour in the wine. Season with salt and pepper. • Cook the pasta in a large pot of salted boiling water until al dente. • Drain and add to the sauce. Sprinkle with parsley and pecorino and serve.

8 oz (250 g) diced pancetta
1/3 cup (90 ml) extra-virgin olive oil
1 large onion, finely chopped
1/4 cup (60 ml) dry white wine
Salt and freshly ground black pepper
1 lb (500 g) dried bucatini, spaghetti, or other dried long pasta shape
2 tablespoons finely chopped fresh parsley
1/3 cup (50 g) freshly grated pecorino cheese

Tuna Sauce
with cherry tomatoes

Sauté the garlic in the oil in a large frying pan over medium heat until pale gold, 2–3 minutes. • Add the tuna and sauté briefly. • Pour in the wine and cook until evaporated. • Add the tomatoes. Season with salt and pepper and simmer for 15 minutes, crushing the tomatoes with a wooden spoon against the sides of the pan. • Cook the pasta in a large pot of salted boiling water until al dente. • Drain and transfer to serving bowls. • Top with the hot sauce. • Sprinkle with parsley and serve immediately.

3 cloves garlic, finely chopped
$1/4$ cup (60 ml) extra-virgin olive oil
8 oz (250 g) tuna, packed in oil, crumbled
$1/2$ cup (125 ml) dry white wine
1 lb (500 g) cherry tomatoes, halved
Salt and freshly ground white pepper
1 lb (500 g) spaghetti or other dried long pasta shape
2 tablespoons finely chopped fresh parsley

SERVES 4–6

PREPARATION 10 min

COOKING 20 min

DIFFICULTY level 1

Radicchio Sauce
with goat cheese

Cook the pasta in a large pan of salted boiling water until al dente. • While the pasta is cooking, sauté the onion in 3 tablespoons of the oil in a large frying pan over medium heat until softened, about 5 minutes. • Add the radicchio and season with salt and pepper. Sauté for a few minutes, then add the beer. When the beer has evaporated, add the goat cheese and milk and stir well. • Drain the pasta well and add to the pan with the sauce. Toss for 1–2 minutes over medium heat. Drizzle with the remaining oil and serve hot.

1 lb (500 g) farfalle or other short pasta shape
1 large onion, thinly sliced
1/4 cup (60 ml) extra-virgin olive oil
2 heads radicchio, cut in strips
Salt and freshly ground black pepper
1/4 cup (60 ml) light beer
4 oz (125 g) soft fresh Italian goat cheese (caprino) (or cream cheese)
2 tablespoons milk

SERVES 4–6

PREPARATION 15 min

COOKING 20 min

DIFFICULTY level 1

Zucchini Sauce
with onion

Heat the oil in a large frying pan over medium heat and sauté the onions and chile for 2–3 minutes. Add the water and simmer over medium-low heat until the water has evaporated. • Add the zucchini and simmer for 10–15 minutes more. Season with salt and pepper. • Meanwhile, cook the pasta in a large pan of salted, boiling water until al dente. • Drain the pasta, not too thoroughly, and add to the pan with the sauce. Toss over high heat for 1–2 minutes. Add the Parmesan and basil and toss again. • Serve hot.

¼ cup (60 ml) extra-virgin olive oil

2 large white onions, thinly sliced in rings

1 fresh red chile, finely chopped

¼ cup (60 ml) cold water

3 large zucchini (courgettes), cut in small cubes

Salt and freshly ground black pepper

1 lb (500 g) whole-wheat (wholemeal) fusilli or other short pasta shape

6 tablespoons freshly grated Parmesan cheese

2–3 tablespoons fresh basil leaves, torn

SERVES 4–6
PREPARATION 30 min + time to prepare pasta
COOKING 30 min
DIFFICULTY level 2

Tomato Sauce
with arugula and parmesan

If using homemade spaghetti, you will need to prepare it the day before you intend to serve this dish. • Sauté the garlic and chile in the oil in a large frying pan over medium heat until the garlic is pale gold, 2–3 minutes. • Stir in the tomatoes and cook for 15 minutes over high heat. • Cook the pasta in a large pot of salted boiling water until al dente. • Drain and add to the sauce. Add the arugula, celery, Parmesan, and parsley. • Toss well and serve hot.

2 cloves garlic, finely chopped
1 dried chile, crumbled
5 tablespoons extra-virgin olive oil
2 cups (500 ml) peeled and chopped tomatoes
1 lb (500 g) homemade spaghetti (see page 35) or storebought whole-wheat (wholemeal) spaghetti
2 large bunches arugula (rocket), finely shredded
1 stalk celery, coarsely chopped
2 oz (60 g) Parmesan cheese, in flakes
1 tablespoon finely chopped fresh parsley

SERVES 4–6

PREPARATION 30 min

COOKING 1 h 30 min

DIFFICULTY level 1

Lamb Sauce
with bell peppers

Sauté the garlic, onion, bay leaves, and lamb in the oil in a large saucepan over medium heat until the meat is browned, 5–10 minutes. • Pour in half the wine and cook until evaporated. • Lower the heat and pour in the remaining wine, cover, and simmer for 40 minutes, or until the meat is almost tender. • Add the bell peppers and tomatoes and cook for 30 minutes more. Season with salt and pepper. • Cook the pasta in a large pot of salted boiling water until al dente. • Drain and add to the sauce. Toss well and serve hot.

2 cloves garlic, lightly crushed but whole
1 large red onion, finely chopped
2 bay leaves
14 oz (400 g) lean lamb, cut into small chunks
5 tablespoons extra-virgin olive oil
$\frac{1}{2}$ cup (125 ml) white wine
1 green bell pepper (capsicum), seeded, and cut into thin strips
1 yellow bell pepper (capsicum), seeded, and cut into thin strips
4 large firm-ripe tomatoes, peeled, seeded, and coarsely chopped
Salt and freshly ground black pepper
1 lb (500 g) cavatappi, fusilli, or other short pasta shape

Onion Sauce
with bread crumbs

Sauté the onion in ¼ cup (60 ml) of the oil in a large frying pan over medium heat until softened, about 5 minutes. • Add the garlic and oregano and sauté for 1 minute. • Season with salt and pepper and remove from the heat. • Toast the bread crumbs in the remaining 2 tablespoons of the oil in a small frying pan over medium heat until golden brown. • Cook the pasta in a large pot of salted boiling water until al dente. • Drain and add to the onion. Sprinkle with the toasted bread crumbs and parsley. Serve hot.

1 large onion, finely chopped
⅓ cup (90 ml) extra-virgin olive oil
2 cloves garlic, finely chopped
1 tablespoon finely chopped fresh oregano
Salt and freshly ground black pepper
6 tablespoons fresh bread crumbs
1 lb (500 g) vermicelli or spaghetti
2 tablespoons finely chopped fresh parsley

Pasta Sauce
with sun-dried tomatoes

Pour ⅓ cup (90 ml) of the oil from the sun-dried tomatoes into a frying pan. Place over medium heat and add the tomatoes. Sauté briefly and season to taste with chile and salt. • Cook the pasta in a large pot of salted boiling water until al dente. Drain and add to the pan. Top with the basil. • Serve hot sprinkled with the cheese.

8 oz (250 g) sun-dried tomatoes packed in oil, finely sliced

Dried chile pepper

Salt

1 lb (500 g) spaghetti or other long pasta shape

Fresh basil leaves, torn

½ cup (60 g) freshly grated caciocavallo or provolone cheese

SERVES 4–6

PREPARATION 30 min + 1 h to drain

COOKING 20 min

DIFFICULTY level 2

Eggplant Sauce
with pine nuts

Place the eggplant slices in a colander and sprinkle with the coarse sea salt. Let drain for 1 hour. • Chop into cubes. • Heat the oil in a large frying pan until very hot. Fry the eggplant in small batches until golden brown, 5–7 minutes per batch. • Broil (grill) the bell peppers until the skins are blackened. Wrap them in a paper bag for 5 minutes, then remove the skins and seeds. Cut into small squares. • Heat 3 tablespoons of the extra-virgin olive oil in a small saucepan and sauté the onion and garlic with a pinch of salt over high heat until golden. Cover and simmer over low heat for 15 minutes. • Toast the pine nuts in a nonstick frying pan over medium heat until golden, 2–3 minutes. • Cook the pasta in a large pot of salted boiling water until al dente. • Drain and transfer to a large serving bowl. Toss well with the fried eggplant, capers, bell peppers, onions, pine nuts, olives, basil, parsley, and oregano and serve hot.

1 large eggplant (aubergine), cut into ½-inch (1-cm) thick slices

Coarse sea salt

2 cups (500 ml) olive oil, for frying

2 tablespoons salt-cured capers, rinsed

2 yellow bell peppers (capsicums)

⅓ cup (90 ml) extra-virgin olive oil

1 medium onion, finely chopped

2 cloves garlic, finely chopped

¼ teaspoon salt

2 tablespoons pine nuts

1 lb (500 g) ditalini or other short pasta shape

1 cup (100 g) green olives, pitted and coarsely chopped

1 small bunch fresh basil, torn

2 tablespoons finely chopped fresh parsley

1 tablespoon finely chopped fresh oregano

Almond Pesto

Chop the almonds finely with the garlic and basil in food processor. • Add the tomato, Parmesan, and ¼ cup (60 ml) of the oil, and mix well. • Cook the pasta in a large pot of salted boiling water until al dente. • While the pasta is cooking, dilute the sauce with 2–3 tablespoons of cooking water. Season with salt. • Drain the pasta and toss with the almond sauce. Drizzle with the remaining oil and serve hot.

8 oz (250 g) blanched almonds
4 cloves garlic
Leaves from 1 small bunch basil
1 large tomato, peeled and diced
¾ cup (90 g) freshly grated Parmesan cheese
5 tablespoons extra-virgin olive oil
1 lb (500 g) linguine or spaghetti
Salt

SERVES 4–6

PREPARATION 10 min

COOKING 15 min

DIFFICULTY level 1

Tuna Sauce
with capers

Rinse the capers under cold running water and cover with fresh water in a small saucepan. Place over medium heat and bring to a boil. Drain the capers, rinse them again, and pat dry on paper towels. • Chop the tuna, capers, mint, and red pepper flakes, if using, in a food processor. • Transfer to a large bowl and mix in the oil. Season with salt. • Cook the pasta in a large pot of salted boiling water until al dente. Add $\frac{1}{4}$ cup (60 ml) of the cooking water to the sauce. • Drain the pasta, reserving a little cooking water, and toss with the tuna sauce, adding more cooking water if needed. Serve hot.

1 cup (100 g) salt-cured capers

8 oz (250 g) tuna packed in oil, drained

Leaves from 1 bunch fresh mint

$\frac{1}{4}$ teaspoon red pepper flakes (optional)

3 tablespoons extra-virgin olive oil

Salt

1 lb (500 g) spaghetti or other long pasta shape

SERVES 4–6

PREPARATION 5 min

COOKING 20 min

DIFFICULTY level 1

Ricotta Sauce
with Italian sausage

Boil the sausage in $\frac{1}{2}$ cup (125 ml) of water in a small saucepan over medium heat for 5 minutes, stirring with a fork occasionally until all of the grease has come out of the sausages. • Remove the pieces of sausage. Place in a bowl and mix in the ricotta. Season with salt and pepper. • Cook the pasta in a large pot of salted boiling water until al dente. • Drain well, reserving 2 tablespoons of the cooking liquid. Add to the bowl with the ricotta, sausage sauce, and cooking liquid. Sprinkle with the pecorino. Toss well and serve hot.

8 oz (250 g) fresh Italian sausage, casing removed and crumbled

14 oz (400 g) fresh ricotta cheese, strained through a fine mesh

Salt and freshly ground white pepper

1 lb (500 g) rigatoni or other short pasta shape

6 tablespoons freshly grated pecorino cheese

SERVES 4–6

PREPARATION 10 min

COOKING 30 min

DIFFICULTY level 1

Zucchini Sauce

Heat the oil in a large deep frying pan until very hot. Fry the zucchini in batches until golden brown, about 5 minutes each batch. Drain well and pat dry on paper towels. Season with salt and cover with a plate to keep them warm. • Cook the pasta in a large pot of salted boiling water until al dente. Drain and sprinkle with pecorino. Top with the fried zucchini, basil, and a drizzle of oil.

1 cup (250 ml) extra-virgin olive oil + extra, to drizzle

1 lb (500 g) zucchini (courgettes), thinly sliced into rounds

Salt

1 lb (500 g) spaghetti or other long or short pasta shape

6 tablespoons freshly grated pecorino cheese

Leaves from 4 bunches fresh basil, torn

SERVES 4–6

PREPARATION 45 min

COOKING 1 h 45 min

DIFFICULTY level 2

Black Sauce

Peel, wash, and cut the squid bodies into rings and cut the tentacles into small pieces. • Sauté the garlic in the oil in a medium saucepan over medium heat until pale gold, 2–3 minutes. Add the squid, parsley, and red pepper flakes. • Cover and simmer over low heat for 45 minutes. • Dissolve the tomato paste in $1/4$ cup (60 ml) of wine and add to the saucepan. Simmer for 20 minutes. • Season with salt and add the hot water. Simmer, covered, for 30 minutes more. • Remove the ink from the sacs, mix with the remaining wine, and add to the sauce a few minutes before serving. • Cook the pasta in a large pot of salted boiling water until al dente. Drain and add to the sauce, mixing well. Serve hot.

1 lb (500 g) squid or cuttlefish, cleaned, with ink sac reserved
2 cloves garlic, finely chopped
$1/4$ cup (60 ml) extra-virgin olive oil
Leaves from 1 small bunch parsley, finely chopped
$1/4$ teaspoon red pepper flakes
2 tablespoons tomato paste (concentrate)
$1/3$ cup (90 ml) dry white wine
Salt
$1/3$ cup (90 ml) hot water
1 lb (500 g) spaghetti or linguine

SERVES 4–6

PREPARATION 30 min

COOKING 20 min

DIFFICULTY level 1

Yogurt Sauce
with avocado

Sauté the garlic and onion in 2 tablespoons of oil in a large frying pan over medium heat until the garlic is pale gold, 2–3 minutes. • Add the wine and cook until evaporated. • Cook the pasta in a large pot of salted boiling water until al dente. • Peel, pit, and dice the avocado. Drizzle with the lemon juice to prevent it from browning. • Beat the yogurt with the remaining oil in a large bowl. Season with salt and pepper. Add the chile, celery, capers, and parsley. • Drain the pasta and toss in the yogurt sauce. Add the onion and avocado, toss again, and serve hot.

2 cloves garlic, finely chopped
1 large onion, chopped
$^1/_4$ cup (60 ml) extra-virgin olive oil
1 tablespoon dry white wine
1 lb (500 g) farfalle, penne, or other short pasta shape
1 ripe avocado
Freshly squeezed juice of 1 lemon
1 cup (250 ml) plain yogurt
Salt and freshly ground black pepper
1 fresh red chile, thinly sliced
1 celery heart, thinly sliced
2 tablespoons salt-cured capers, rinsed
1 tablespoon finely chopped fresh parsley

SERVES 4–6

PREPARATION 25 min

COOKING 30 min

DIFFICULTY level 1

Cherry Tomato

sauce with pesto

Preheat the oven to 350°F (180°C/gas 4). • Place the cherry tomatoes on a baking sheet, sliced side up, and drizzle with 2 tablespoons of oil. Lightly dust with salt and pepper. • Bake for 15 minutes. • Chop the basil, Parmesan, garlic, almonds, and remaining oil in a food processor until smooth. Season with salt and pepper. • Meanwhile, cook the pasta in a large pan of salted boiling water until al dente. • Drain well and place in a heated serving dish. • Add the pesto and baked tomatoes and toss gently. • Serve hot.

1½ lb (750 g) cherry tomatoes, cut in half

⅓ cup (90 ml) extra-virgin olive oil

Salt and freshly ground white pepper

2 oz (60 g) fresh basil

½ cup (60 g) freshly grated Parmesan cheese

2 cloves garlic, peeled

1½ oz (45 g) peeled almonds

1 lb (500 g) linguine, spaghetti, or other long pasta shape

Index

Copyright © 2009 by McRae Books Srl

This English edition first published in 2009

Pasta Sauces

was created and produced by McRae Books Srl

Via del Salviatino 1 – 50016 Fiesole, (Florence) Italy

info@mcraebooks.com

Publishers: Anne McRae and Marco Nardi

Project Director: Anne McRae

Design: Sara Mathews

Text: McRae Books archive

Editing: Carla Bardi

Photography: Studio Lanza (Lorenzo Borri, Cristina Canepari, Ke-ho Casati, Mauro Corsi, Gil Gallo, Leonardo Pasquinelli, Gianni Petronio, Stefano Pratesi, Sandra Preussinger)

Home Economist: Benedetto Rillo

Artbuying: McRae Books

Layouts: Aurora Granata, Filippo Delle Monache, Davide Gasparri

Repro: Fotolito Raf, Florence

ISBN 978-88-6098-082-3

Printed and bound in China